Cameos for the Journey

By Carol Jean Wright

Edited by David E. Johnson

7/06

To Barbara —
Find joy on
your spiritual journey —
much aloha,
Carol Jean

Acknowledgments

On my spiritual journey so many people have played a large part. You are all part of my 'Ohana" (Hawaiian for family). I hesitate to mention any for fear of excluding some. I am grateful for my mother and father and all the early lessons that they taught me. My sister Bernie actually did more to raise me than my mother. Thank you for the childhood we shared and for the Saturday morning phone calls.

Hopefully, I have been part of your spiritual journey or will be now. Thank you, for the hard lessons and the sweet lessons. I have to thank my editor, friend, soul mate and husband Dr. David E. Johnson for all you did and all that you are.

My photography is scattered throughout this book. The cover is also one of my photos.

Contents

Magic in Beginning	1
Learn the Lesson	2
Learn from Your Pets	3
Just Breathe	4
Prejudice Takes Many Forms	5
The "S" Turn	6
The Pity Party	7
Judging Backfires	8
Divine Order Is	9
The Law	10
Wee Small Voice	11
No Spot	12
"P.A.T."	13
Pray First not Last	14
Song From the Fronds	15
Positive Thoughts	16
Forgiveness is a Must	17
Live_____.	18
Lukewarm Doesn't Cut It	19
Trails on the Path	20
Morning Gifts	21
Drop the Load	22
Rich Memories	23
Just Give the Gift	24
Rainbows All Around	25
Dancing Lupines	26
Pet Losses	27
More Will Be Revealed	28
Use the New Gadgets	29
Just Let Go	30
Go With the Flow	31
God's Angel	32
Coming Home	33
Mourning the Past	34

Erase the Old Tapes	35
There is No Try	36
Just Do It	37
Terminal Potlucks	38
God's Report Card	39
What is Grace?	40
Pick Up Your Mat	41
Use Your Senses	42
It's History	43
Love of Life	44
Alligators of the Mind	45
Wonders Abound	46
Extraordinary	47
Woulda, Shoulda, Coulda	48
Sonlight	49
Is That It?	50
180 Degree Turn	51
Watch for Monkey Wrenches	52
Nothing is Lost in Spirit	53
JC Doesn't Play	54
One Liners	55
Laughter Gets You Through	56
Be Gentle	57
Thanks for the Message	58
Wake Up	59
Beauty at the Ballet	60
He Watches Me	61
Dump the Baggage	62
A New Page	63
Full Computer	64
Chose Happy	65
Breathe the Smell	66
Carry Twigs	67
Slow Down	68
Plant Seeds	69
Slowly Die	70

Different Strokes

"Magic In Beginning"

Commitment is a strange and funny process. For some time I had thought of writing a book. On my sojourn around North America I thought this might be a good time. So I started this book and had written about ten of the short stories before I told my husband. I didn't share it with him because that would put it out in the universe. I also had not told him to keep it a secret.

So the night he announced to his sister that I was writing a book, I felt these strange sensations come over me. First I thought this is my secret. Second I was filled with a sense that this wasn't just a dream but could actually happen. Thirdly I was ready to kill David because he had put it out there into the universe and had not kept my secret. Not to worry; he is still alive today.

Finally I remembered what Goethe had said about the universe coming to help in all forms when we set our intention to our commitment. WOW. The creativity started to flow at a much deeper level. Everywhere I turned there were new growth stories coming into my life.

Here was the person writing that had been told she could never write. Here was the person that was ready to put her *fear* aside and BEGIN. Fear being false evidence appearing real. There really is magic in BEGINNING.

"Learn the Lesson"

How do we learn our lessons when our heart is involved? There is a joy in learning to let go when things are not going the way we want. Most times in my life I had been the 'dumper' in relationships not the 'dumpee'. I was going to ministerial school and I had been dumped.

This particular night I was within ten blocks from his home. I thought I would drive by and see if he was home. I asked myself what is your purpose? I didn't intend to stop. If his car was there I would be upset, if there was another car there I would be upset, or if his car wasn't there I would be upset. For once in my life I took charge of the event. My purpose was to not do something that would make me upset. I realized before the fact that I was creating a no win situation.

I thought 'Why don't I just take the tire jack out of the trunk and beat myself over the head.' If I was into inflicting pain, that was very effective.

I was in charge of my emotions. I could be "at choice" even in matters of the heart. I drove home thinking about how I had taken back my power. I started to laugh all the way home. Thank you God for my awareness of your presence at times like this. Thank you God for lessons as the 'dumpee'.

"Learn From Your Pets"

Dimi, my cat, thinks mornings are the greatest time in the world. She thinks nothing of causing the household to wake so she can be put out. What is it that is so special about the dawn hours? She just sits there so contented to look around. What is it she sees? This morning I decided to stay up and that was quite a gift. I decided to write about the moment.

Looking out at the dawn breaking, the semi-leafless trees were dark silhouettes in the morning light. A sliver of a moon was shining brightly as a jet vapor passed beneath it with a bright pink trail. Indistinguishable black birds fly across the sky as lone leaves settling to the rust carpet of leaves already laid down. Slowly the color begins to change from the horizon up in tones of golden and light purplish rays.

This is what Dimi likes. This is the time to be grateful for the beginning of a new day. The song 'Morning has Broken' comes to mind. This is the day the Lord has made. This is a "Sonday". It is in fact a Sunday also. This is a day to be aware of the newness around me; a day to watch and see what a beloved pet can teach me. Thank you Dimi for being a beacon of God's light. Thank you for being a curious cat, exploring the wonders of the morning.

" Just Breathe"

While my husband, David and I are on this 9-month sojourn around North America, the question arises who ministers to the ministers. We have gone to various Unity Churches throughout Canada and the USA. Each church has its own personality; each church works in some way or another. Sometimes it all comes together like it finally did one Sunday morning.

We had decided to go to our third church in the DC area while we were at Andrews Air Force base. I was sure I knew how to come out the back gate and get to the church. My map reading was off a bit and at the time for the church to begin we were going the wrong way on a freeway. I remembered I had the cell phone and called the church. Lucky because by now the two ministers were yelling at each other plus the church had changed location some three months before.

With the right directions we arrived at the church 15 minutes late and the regular minister was out sick. My beloved was steaming to say the least. I whispered in my holy voice "Let's be open to the miracles; we are here by Divine appointment."

The speaker was an old friend, the music was awesome, the message was good, someone from David's seminary days was there, and on and on. *__The lesson is breathe and watch for God's gift.__*

"Prejudice Takes Many Forms"

While we were visiting a Unity Church on our 9-month RV trip around North America, I learned a very good lesson. The church was integrated and the people really were quite colorblind. The lesson was that prejudice takes many forms. The music director was someone I knew and had taken voice lessons from a long time ago.

When it was time for the soloist, she was nowhere in sight so he decided to fill in with piano music. While he was doing this, a street person appeared. This was after 9-11-01 and she was a bag lady. There were many different reactions. The speaker for the Sunday thought of taking her out. He said something to the pastor's wife and she responded "let's pray".

David, my husband, was going to go up and sit with her. She went up and took the mike. All of a sudden it came to me this might be the special music. But no, this lady had to be a totally beaten down street person. After the entire church had judged her, she began to sing. She had written the song herself and no one, not even the music director knew what she was going to do.

Socially economic difference is just another form of prejudice; the need to say" I must be better than you because I am richer or smarter." Thanks to the soloist, the whole church had a lesson that morning, even if she had been a street person, which she wasn't. She was a child of God.

"The 'S' Turn"

While living in Hawaii I joined a rough water swim group. What a wonderful time that turned out to be. We lived on the 10th floor of a condo right on the ocean beneath Diamond Head. The area in front of this building was one of the world's greatest swimming areas. It was inside a reef with one slight 's' turn going out to the open ocean. This was fine on calm clear days but when the ocean would kick up it would be quite difficult. The waves could throw you on the reef on either side and the sand on the bottom would make the visibility poor.

It was during times like this that I would look out and down and think I'm not going to swim this morning. Yet from up above it was easy to see the way the 's' turn snaked out to the open ocean. I would get my suit on and go down and do my stretching with the group, get in the water and promptly lose sight of the way through the channel.

The lesson that came to me was how easy it is to see the way when we see the bigger picture or when we can rise above the problem. In life when the waves are crashing over head and we feel like we are being thrown about, step back and see the bigger picture. It isn't always easy to do this but it sure is better then drowning in the problem. The way through the 's' turn problem, no matter what it is ,is from above. Thank you God.

"The Pity Party"

My first Unity minister, mentor, friend and teacher was Amalie Frank. She was ordained when she was sixty-seven. This was a time of real growth in my life thanks to Amalie.

One Christmas, which happened to fall on a Sunday, Amalie offered to lend me her car if I would take her to the airport. I didn't have a car at the time and so the few days she was going to be visiting her children was a gift from God. After church I drove her out to the airport. This was the perfect time to tell her all the sad and sorrowful things that were going on in my life.

Here I was on the East Coast and all my family were on the West Coast. She said right in the middle of one of my sad tales, "It sounds like you are having a 'pity party' to me." After a moment or two I thought I'd start again from a different angle. Again she said "Sounds like you have the PLOM disease." I asked what that was and she said, "Poor Little Old Me."

I was so upset that as we got to the airport I thought I would just slow down the car and push her out. She got out of the car and said, "Merry Christmas Amalie's hard love was the greatest gift anyone had ever given me. I was "at choice" that day and **I GOT IT**.

I could choose to have whatever kind of Christmas I chose. Before the day was over I had created a <u>Christmas to remember</u>. Thank you God and Amalie.

"Judging Backfires"

Be careful what you ask for. I was asking God to make my lessons shorter and easier. I was living in Hawaii and had returned to the mainland to see my aging mother and I had brought pictures to show her. The pictures were quite good of me, I thought. She was looking through them and asked who was that. I couldn't believe it. My mother had gotten to the point she couldn't even recognize her own daughter.

Hours later I was back at my sister's home where I was staying during my visit. My sister and I have always been exceptionally close. I shared with her about the pictures and mother. I was concerned; did she feel mother was failing that fast? She said she hadn't noticed any great change.

My sister then brought out some pictures she had taken to share with me. My son, Ryan had been living with her while he was going to college. I was looking at the pictures and I asked "Who is that?" She looked at me rather strangely and said "That is your son." The picture was a reflection of Ryan in a mirror and I didn't recognize my own son.

After all the judgments about my mother's aging process, here I was. I really had to laugh. Not only was the lesson faster than usual, but I really got it. The time I waste by judging, judging, judging. God really does have a sense of humor. So be careful what you ask for.

"Divine Order Is"

There is a fascination about the way we learn or get a new idea. I once read that we repeat 99 % of our thoughts everyday and only 1% is new thoughts or ideas. Part of the growth process on my spiritual journey is to be aware of the 1%.

When I first heard the words Divine Order, I thought how wonderful. WOW! I need do nothing but pray for Divine Order.

For years when any challenge, crisis, or concern would come into my life I would pray for Divine Order. One day a light went off and I thought I don't have to pray for Divine Order because Divine Order just is. **This was big**. I had no control over Divine Order; all I had to do was raise my consciousness. This concept is easy when everything is going smoothly.

The point I had to learn was to remember this as quickly as possible during the rocky times. As I ranked the three C's,(challenges, concerns, and crisis) it became clear it was easiest with concerns. If some challenge arose it seemed to take longer and a full-blown crisis might pass without remembering my "new thought" that everything is in fact in Divine Order.

The lesson is to reach this higher level of knowing as fast as possible because with the knowing comes the peace. I need do nothing. God is in charge of my life and affairs and only good can come to me.

"The Law"

The road to ministerial school has many routes and growth opportunities. My friend Mary and I got the calling about the same time. They only take a limited predetermined number, so it feels like a competition while deep inside you know there is no competition with God. The number invited after applications, psychological testing, and letters from ministers and prerequisite schooling exceeds those finally accepted. Mary and I both applied and were invited for interviews. This next step involved more testing and two forty-five minute interviews with two ministers from the field.

The schedule came out. You dressed in your Sunday best and nervously arrived at the first interview. There was always a lot of late night quarter-backing about what questions would be asked. Mary went before I did to the first interview. Of course each interview was entirely different depending on which ministers you had and how God worked through them. After she came out we asked what the questions were.

One of the questions was "What is the law ?" Mary looked out the window and asked them to repeat the question? She finally answered, " I don't suppose it is 55 MPH." Mary got in that year and I did not. They never asked me that question the following year.

We later learned the right answer: "Thoughts held in mind produce after their kind." This is the powerful Law of Mind Action.

"Wee Small Voice"

My friend Mary and I were at Unity Village going to the Continuing Education Program. We both were there for a full month and had no car. The school was broken into two two-week periods. During the weekend separating the two periods we had the opportunity to go to a yoga class down on the Kansas City Plaza. We jumped at the chance because it would give us time to pick up a few items we needed plus have lunch.

We were very aware of the 'wee small voice'. This is the voice in each of us that guides and directs us. This is the voice that sorts out our old beliefs and opens us to the new. It is very easy to question if this voice is from God or from our ego.

On the Plaza was a wonderful Saks Fifth Avenue store. We went in and tried on hats. I convinced Mary that a big purple velvet hat was definitely "her". I bought a small knit beret. As we were leaving the store a loud speaker came on and said, "Return to the counter you just left." We were talking and laughing and again the same message came on, "Return to the counter you just left". We finally realized that the message was meant for us. The sensor on my hat had not been removed!

Laughing as we left the store, we wondered how we would ever hear the 'wee small voice' if in fact we couldn't even discern when a loud speaker was talking to us.

"No Spot"

My father would say, "You bring your own fun to the party." I grew up knowing and remembering this saying. Through the years I finally got to understand most of them. One liners are the most help in the midst of the biggest issues.

For many years in my life I expected someone else to create the celebrations around my birthday. I always was disappointed in some way. One year I went to Hong Kong with two other women. This was the year I was "four dozen". I had never heard this term until my birthday that year in Hong Kong. It was a birthday to remember.

As I approached my sixtieth birthday I wondered what one does when they are five dozen? My husband, David arranged for the rental of Silcox Hut. This hut is located a mile above Timberline Lodge on Mt Hood. There was a small select group from all around the country. We went up by snow cat or chairlift and stayed the night. The next morning was Sunday and we had a spiritual celebration.

It was z celebration to remember beyond the next dozen years. The mountain loomed in its majestic wonders right outside the windows. Our souls had come to the mountaintop. It is important to take the time to celebrate life on a mountaintop, always remembering the one liners that help us on this spiritual journey. One liners like "There is no spot where God is not." "Peace be still." and certainly "You bring your own fun to the party."

" P.A.T."

One of the greatest ways for me to come back to a peaceful and contented place is to remember PAT. That stands for praise, appreciation, and thanksgiving. In the fall of the year just before winter and the start of a period of less light, it is life transforming to remember PAT.

Praise causes people to grow. In my life, simple words like 'I am proud of you' have changed my life. There are times in our lives when we need to encourage others to play big. During these times praise might help someone find what is solely theirs to do to change human kind.

Appreciation is more what we do after the fact. This is important in all relationships. We must remember to appreciate the little things others do.

Thanksgiving is just that, giving thanks. As we take the time to look around us and note the smallest wonders of this earth, we are transformed with thanksgiving. God gives us gifts everyday in the form of sunrises and sunsets. The gifts are giving of good health, prosperity, imagination, and so many more. All we have to do is look around and see the presents in the present.

As we remember PAT, just pat your heart. This is a simple gesture which anchors our thoughts of praise, appreciation, and thanksgiving in a deeper way.

"Pray First not Last"

During our great swing around North America in our motor home, we spent Thanksgiving with our minister friends Pat and LeRoy. It was a wonderful time. While going to seminary we had had a remarkable Thanksgiving in their new home. We had prayed and did a blessing for their new home.

This year also had many highlights. The two that come to mind are the blessing before dinner and the ride to see the Christmas lights along the ocean after dinner. The blessing was new and wonderful to us. Under each napkin on the plates were four popcorn kernels. Each person would take one and say one thing they were thankful for. We went around the table each taking one kernel at a time. Pat's mother lives with them and at one point she asked "When **do** we eat?"

After dinner, seven of us were off in a van to see the lights. The line was long and the van started to heat up. LeRoy would start and stop it, so needless to say the sightseeing trip was a little hairy. Everyone could feel the tension except Pat's mom. After about thirty minutes I looked at Pat and asked if she had said a prayer yet. The answer was no. So we both put our hands out in front of us and silently said a prayer. Pat's mom wanted to know what we were doing. "Oh nothing Mom", was the reply. Mom put her hands out and helped us.

The question here is, "How fast do we remember to go to God in prayer?"

"Song from The Fronds"

Another New Year has dawned in much the same way as it has for all of my years on this planet and yet----. I could look out and see a country on the edge of war on two fronts, unusual weather patterns and global warming, economic uncertainty on all levels from city, county, state and nationally, plus individual losses of pension and retirement funds and yet----.

The sun was dawning in the desert in bright reds and pinks. The mountains were standing as magnificent and stately as the day they were formed. They were looking down with a protective, caring and loving gaze at the valley below. In a palm tree a huge flock of black birds was lined on the fronds as if an aviary choirmaster had arranged them. The birds were singing the same song but the tenors were lined on the left and the sopranos on the right, the altos in the middle and the basses were on the lower rungs where the fronds use to be.

As my walk came to a close, my mind had let go of concerns of this New Year. In place was a deep thanksgiving for all the things in this world that really needed to fill the frond rungs of my mind. Thank you God for the gentle reminder that what is appearing 'out there' isn't what it is all about. The peace comes from 'in here'. This coming year can hold many things but my job is to hold the higher watch and sing praises from the highest rungs.

"Positive Thoughts"

Today I want to watch myself and see how often I have a negative thought. Studies tell us we use only ten percent of our minds. If eight percent is on negative thoughts, that doesn't leave much for positive thoughts.

I love the cartoon that says "God, I haven't offended anyone today, I have been watching to keep negative thoughts out of my head. I have not had one judgment or experienced any anger. Of course I am not out of bed yet." It does seem to work pretty well until we start to deal with family, friends, or committees.

So far today I had a chance to look at my thought patterns on the tennis court. If I don't let an opponent camp in my head, I am doing a negative number on my tennis skills. If I focus and tell myself that 'I am a good tennis player; just enjoy the moment.', my game improves.

Paul tells us in the Bible to think about the good, the beautiful and the positive. He says, "Think on these things." If we are Truth students and know this then why is it so easy to think "less than" of others and mostly ourselves? For the rest of this day, try something with me. See if we can go two hours without a negative thought or judgment. Be aware of how strong our thoughts are in creating our day. As You were in Paul, God, let me be aware of You today in my thoughts and actions.

"Forgiveness is a Must"

Once a year when we were snow birding in the south, my sister would come for a week to visit. It seems like we always had such an opportunity to look at the dynamics between us. I believe we are here on this special spiritual journey to grow and to learn new lessons about love and forgiveness. It doesn't matter our age or how long the relationship, there is always another level of forgiveness we can reach.

The bible tells us that we must forgive 70 times 7. That is just on one issue, not on one person. It seems we have certain issues with special people and we get to look at them year after year. Just when we might think that we have finally grown through a certain issue, it comes back and we grow some more. I am sure I have never forgiven 490 times on anything.

The faster we can come to a resolve on any issue the sooner we will experience peace and serenity. I don't know about you but the energy it takes to look at our own "stuff" takes a lot of time. To experience this thing called Heaven here on earth means finding peace and serenity in all our relationships. So next year I will see if there has been any growth in love and forgiveness on this wonderful spiritual journey called life. It is time to find the joy that is meant for each of us RIGHT NOW.

"Live _____."

Half measures give us nothing. It is so easy to live in half measures. Each day offers us the opportunity to live "full out or sort of ". Lance Armstrong tells us to 'Live Strong'. It is much easier to just go along with the everyday safety of ho-hum. Indifference seems to seep in as we do each task.

When I get ready to do the housework, my pattern is hit and miss. On a day when I do the deepest level of cleaning, the time flies. The feeling of contentment in just smelling and looking at the finished product is awesome. Half measures don't give the pleasure that 'full out' at the top of the game does.

This seems to be a pattern in my life; Don't give it your all because if you come up short you won't look good, or you will have to do it again as well as you did the first time, and a thousand justifications of why half measures have value. Trust me they don't have value. The feeling that comes when I let my Brother Lawrence out in the everyday tasks is so great. The time goes by in a meditative state plus the payoffs are so much greater than doing things slip shod.

The tool here is to ask God to reveal when the 'half measures' start to muddy up the joy of giving something your all. This applies to all areas of life. Living full makes the journey so much more exciting. Put what ever you want as the second word: live <u>big</u>, live <u>full</u>, live <u>joyously</u>; the point is to REALLY live.

"Lukewarm Doesn't Cut It"

We put a circulating water system in our house so you don't have to waste ten gallons of water getting to hot. The down side of that is that the cold is always lukewarm to warm. I like hot or cold. Lukewarm doesn't work for me. There is always a trade-off in life. You don't have to wait for hot water in the shower but you have to have cold water in the refrigerator at all times.

It is not a big thing. In other areas of my life I do "lukewarm" a lot. Putting this book together was one of those times. I knew the results I wanted and yet connecting the dots was hard. I was lukewarm. Not committed to hot or cold. Actually I was lukewarm in my thinking. What is my next step? Right now, get quiet, ask God for guidance and direction, write it down, and just choose "hot".

In Revelations a message to Sardis says, "Up on your feet! Take a deep breath! Maybe there's life in you yet. But I wouldn't know it by looking at your busy work, nothing of God's work has been completed. Your condition is desperate." It is time to get hot about what ever is yours to do. Start today by taking a look at your dreams, your hopes, your goals. For God's sake do not be lukewarm because God can only do for you what He can do through you.

"Trails on the Path"

While walking my daily route on a paved road that had long been closed, the after slide of a slug tailings was glistening in the morning sun. It was obvious that the slug made so many criss-crosses and meanderings that he often didn't make it across the road before a jogger or walker had inadvertently ended his life.

I couldn't help but wonder how much this was like my own life. There have been so many detours and side trips on this journey. Even when I got serious about my spiritual journey it was anything but a straight upward and forward line. I must admit that there were certainly moments when the path had some glistening moments along with the many dead ends and attitude directional changes.

It is important at these moments when God talks to us through nature to be grateful for the insight. Actually I was aware of the slow plodding of the tortoise but in my mind they just want slow and mostly straight. They didn't seem to leave their trail on the concrete blackboard of life.

On my future morning walks I can't say how many times I would take a little side step so the slug could live another day. It was easy to behold the Christ in the slug on the road as I was walking home to spread my slug bait. I must remember I am still evolving, also. Maybe next year I'll buy plants that the slugs don't consider their 'Godiva chocolate'.

"Morning Gifts"

Fall is coming to the mountain. I sit at this window lots of mornings and don't see anything new. Today I decided to wake up and look for something I hadn't seen or noticed for some time. On my morning walks I realize if I just turn around and walk the same course in a different direction the things I see are very different.

Before I describe what God has painted and arranged outside my window this morning, I want to acknowledge a speaker I heard recently. He was a former Catholic priest and mystic from the more gray and damp part of Ireland. He never walks the dunes but what he sees a new and wonderful surprise from God. Wake up and smell the coffee. I live in one of the most beautiful parts of the country during the summer months. Each day I challenge myself to see some new awesome gem that God has awakened me to this day.

My window view is my gift today. The fall sunlight is different. The air feels like hints of fall. The changing maple leaves are backlit with the morning light. The breeze is gently filtering the light dancing from leaf to leaf. The geranium leaves have such big veins with the sunlight behind them. Red geraniums in the window boxes look like high alpine cottages. The screen that will be soon replaced with a window, has a wee spider scampering across the vast voids. WOW God; thanks for my awakening to your gifts.

"Drop the Load"

My friend Dee and I walk each weekday morning. At least we do when we are both on the mountain. These walks have led to some deep talks and revelations. One day we were talking about wanting to help our adult children. Actually to wave a magic wand over their problems and help them not have to go through some of the minefields, errors and mistakes that we experienced at their age.

Some times these issues can be about control or the inability to let go. As we were deep in discussion about how energy draining and useless this habit seems to be, we spotted a slug moving along the road. Somehow the slug had this most lovely array of fir needles and other things it had picked up along the way. We both began to laugh.

This was like the parent that takes on all the problems and gets slower and heavier with each worry or concern. The energy it takes to drag our load takes away from our good. Like the slug there seems to be cosmic glue that is quite difficult to be rid of. I am sure that the seasons will help the slug let go of his load but what is it that will help us?

I believe it is God showing us this wonderful lesson from nature that will let us release a little more each time. We can love our children and be there for them but let them figure out how to drop the fir needles along the journey.

"Rich Memories"

God's gifts come in the form of rich memories. While doing a wedding in a country setting, I was filled with rushes of beautiful memories. I also had the opportunity to view another memory with new eyes.

I walked out to this old barn that had been cleared of animals for many years. They used it as a backup area in case of rain. On the back wall were many old feed sacks nailed up. My mother would take the feed sacks that were cotton and had a floral print and make pillowcases and tea towels. Once she made me a shirt and because of the lowly place it had come from, I never liked it. How I wished I could have thanked my mother again for her many gifts! The years had given me the opportunity to be grateful and see things in a different way.

I had arrived early for the rehearsal at this B & B called "The Farm". The garden was most inviting also as it was a mix of early fall flowers and vegetables. I picked some orange cherry tomatoes and popped them in my mouth. Instantly the wonderful times of walking in my father's garden came into my mind. On a hot summer day I would take the salt shaker and pick a sun warmed tomato and have a feast.

I was so filled with a sense of gratitude for the gift of memories and the joy of continuing to walk in my Father's garden.

"Just Give the Gift"

Once a friend said to me "I made $500 today." and I immediately wanted to know how. He said a friend of his wanted to borrow $1,000 and he only lent him $500. This seemed so *enormous* to me. What a lesson! He was giving a gift not expecting to get it back. I was never going to forget this.

Years later a friend was not working and he mentioned he would go to see his children but he didn't have the money. I did, so I lent it to him with a signed note. He took the trip and returned and I saw less and less of him. I would run into him at church from time to time. I was losing so much energy over this issue, it was ridiculous. I would ask him for the money and once he actually gave me a small amount toward the note.

One Sunday he arrived at church wearing an awesome pair of new cowboy boots. I could see red. I needed to let this go for my own mental health.

I had to do so much work around this issue. When you lend someone money, treat it like a gift. The lesson I thought I had learned earlier came back in a different form so I could learn it at a deeper level. Over the years the way abundance has filled my life has come in so many ways. God is good in giving lessons and abundant gifts. When one door closes another opens.

"Rainbows All Around"

We don't always know the plan. David and I were visiting the Island of Kauai. We decided to go for a helicopter ride. If you have lived on the Islands for any time, you read about the crashes of these sightseeing rides. So it was with a little apprehension that I had made up my mind to go. We had a three o'clock time. The car ride to the helicopter pad was about 45 minutes from where we were staying. The skies kept getting darker and darker the closer we got to the airport. The winds came up outside, as well as in my mind.

God, I don't think I want to do this in this weather. What if they won't give your money back if you cancel? The winds in my mind were quite strong.

We arrived in a downpour. They announced that all the rest of the day's flights were cancelled. Thank you God. They told us to come back tomorrow. The next day was pristine. The sky was the deepest blue, the ocean in a greener hue. We took off with another couple in the back, the pilot on my left and David on my right. We had headsets on because of the noise. It was awesome. All the waterfalls were spilling very full. At one point the pilot came in next to a falls and the blades made little rainbows all around. Just as we broke over the ridge into Waimea Canyon, the pilot had timed it so 'Grand Canyon Suite' was playing through our headsets.

My eyes filled with happy tears as I experienced a closeness to my God.

"Dancing Lupines"

Nature has always made me realize just how wonderful our Master Gardener is. One of the most wonderful times was on the side of Mt Hood. I was on a short overnight golf trip with two friends. We were looking out the windows toward the mountain on this August afternoon. There were skiers skiing on the glacier above an alpine meadow. The meadows were full of lupines and the wind was blowing them in wonderful patterns. At that moment it was my "fields of shining grain". There were also splotches of Red Indian paint brush mixed in. The movement was like a great dance of Mother Nature.

I was having an euphoric moment. The feelings of connectedness with God, my friends and the earth were beautifully interwoven. All of my senses were on high alert and I was so aware of how awesome life is.

Fast forward many years as David and I drove up to Mt Hood to see the moon rise. We knew the approximate time but were not sure of the exact direction. We were in the location looking at the ending pinks of a grand sunset in the early dusk. To the right of the mountain the moon broke out in all its wonder. Now I felt like the Master Architect had done it again. God was talking to me through nature. How could anyone every ask,"Is there a God?" My answer would be, go to the mountain and watch the sunset, the dance of the lupines and the moonrise. God is there.

"Pet Losses"

Two different friends lost their beloved dogs recently. The dogs were both about thirteen years old. It seems like such a short time to spread unconditional love on this planet. I couldn't help but look at my beloved Joy Luck and Dim Sum, a dog and cat, and wonder how long they will be with us. These are my first indoor pets.

We had all kinds of farm animals but they were always kept outside. It is easier to keep an animal outside your heart when they live 'outside.' The day I got an email from friends sharing how they had taken Lady out to a grassy knoll to put her to sleep, I sobbed. They hadn't wanted her to have to be on a cold metal table.

When I was walking yesterday I ran into one of the owners of Missy. I didn't know quite what to say. I started telling her a story about my first death out of ministerial school. It had been a request to do a memorial for a pet. I was trying to show how much I knew about the pet grieving process. I actually showed how little I knew about just being there for someone in times of deep sorrow.

God, may I always remember in the future that during times of condolence no one wants to hear a story; only be held and heard. The other thing I must remember is what great teachers our pets can be as they silently teach us how to love unconditionally.

"More Will Be Revealed"

Currently in the morning paper there was an article about 'proving Einstein was right about the speed of gravity'. This is hard for me to get my mind around. Is it important that I completely understand this issue? Maybe no! I was so excited by this as I knew it was about light and God working through people.

The intellectual mind that is able to think something like that is awesome. Einstein was way ahead in his thinking to be able to conceive of this concept. The scientist that arrived at the process of measuring this at least has the latest scientific tools derived through Creative Mind.

Divine Mind was present in all of these revelations. I think it is important for me to understand not necessarily the scientific process, but that we don't always have to prove all the innate things we know. On this spiritual journey it is the trail of learning not the end product.

My husband, David, loves to say, "More will be revealed." The important aspect is that we stay open so more can be revealed. I like the practice of asking God each morning, "What is mine to do this day?" I don't have to totally understand each moment <u>*because more will be revealed*</u>. I am not in charge of anyone else's emotions, feelings, or actions.

Things I know this morning: there is an awesomely constructed universe: with an awesomely constructed mind in each of us; and God is present in all of it.

"Use the New Gadgets"

It is very exciting to live in the age of computers and digital cameras. Just about the time I finally mastered the VCR along comes a whole lot of new things to get my mind around.

There was a time at the very beginning of all of this that I hoped that I wouldn't have to tax my brain with all this new material. Could I get by without learning how to use a computer? I certainly could get by with the typewriter. It seems so complicated. I was working on the campaign for the governor elect of Oregon at the time. I would watch the word processing person in awe knowing I would never be able to do that. All the time wondering why I would even want to.

As I watch the words fill this page, go backwards, forwards, edit, use spell check, cut, paste, and on and on, I was grateful I live in this age. I now have a digital camera and while it still has 99% more capacity than I am using, I can see the potential.

On this spiritual journey, so many times I can see the potential for others but not always for myself. I can see the power of Divine Mind working in those that created all of these gadgets. I chose this day to see how Divine Mind works in my mind and how to use these tools to a greater percentage. I am open to recording words and pictures in ways that express my creativity. I am open to the joy in the creating.

"Just Let Go"

A small group of us were sitting around eating hot dogs before a movie. One man shared that he was not ashamed to say he had a phobia of snakes. The conversation turned to rats and mice. Most of the stories were about dark experiences and deep fear. Always ending in the horrible way they had killed these creatures.

After a certain period of time my husband and I tried to change the subject. We actually said 'Let's move this conversation to a higher, brighter place.' They wanted to tell a few more stories. The group was enjoying talking about their fears, phobias and how they killed the enemy. There was no desire to change a belief or work on a phobia but only to have it be an in-depth part of their story.

I begin to wonder what it is in my story that might need to be changed. I am aware of the power of the spoken word. Each time I tell my same negative story or reinforce the fear or phobia, it is a way to hold on to something which is serving me in some way. This seems like such an important matter in the way each of us fits into the universe of God's plan.

I am wondering if there is some correlation between how we must chop up snakes and how threatened we are by people who want to move to a more positive ground. It is time for me to stop telling stories about negative happenings in my life. God help me to see the bigger picture. God help me to shine light on my shortcomings, phobias, and fears.

"Go With the Flow"

It is raining on the RV roof. Outside of the windows the mighty McKenzie River is flowing full and rushing to its appointment down stream. It probably doesn't know it will have its mouth at the Willamette River joining there and turning from a westerly flow to a northerly flow. The Willamette takes the McKenzie plus many other tributaries to the Columbia where it turns west again and flows to the sea.

God has created such an incredible water shed in the Pacific Northwest. The clear sparkling water of the McKenzie is so different from the Missouri and Mississippi rivers. On our big nine-month sojourn across this country we went out of our way to see the tidal change at the Bay of Fundy. The winds were strong and the great muddy reversal of the waters didn't happen. What a disappointment! There is such a great variety of ways a drop of water can live its life. Always it is moving back to its source and beginning again.

Can I compare my journey with that of a river? I am never sure exactly when my spiritual journey might take a huge detour. I do know that I sometimes meander and sometimes rush in my quest for the source. Sometimes there is a drought and other times my river flows full. Sometimes there might be a root dam in my path. The solution is to just enjoy the float down the river always remembering He is at the helm of the boat. Thank you God for all of your creations.

"God's Angel"

Some people believe in angels and some don't. If you do believe in them you are never sure in what form they will appear. My husband David and I were going back to revisit a natural hot springs in Oregon that we had found on our honeymoon some ten years before. The hot springs are not very well marked because they have had problems with vandalism and various other issues.

We drove to this Hot Springs off of the McKenzie River. When we arrived we sized the parking area up and there were two young men. David went over and asked them some questions and made eye contact with them thinking this was some form of insurance. We don't have to look in a mirror to see how 'establishment' we must appear and yet here we are looking for a Hot Springs where suits are optional.

We were parked beside a ranger's truck. I had said a prayer and surrounded our car in God's light and love. We walked the short distance up to the pools. They were blocked off for some work so we couldn't go in them. Very disappointed, we walked back to our car. Both David and I were relieved to see the car in tack.

A man came over out of his camper and told us that he heard the boys talking about putting a rock through our windshield. He had surprised them when he appeared from his camper. **He was our angel**. God had sent someone to watch over our car with light and love. Thank you God.

"Coming Home"

The conclusion of a dream is such a sweet period. David and I have just completed a 12,000 mile nine month swing around North America. It seems so important to have some kind of ritualistic ending. This morning in our readings we read, "***God, help me fully embrace and finish my ending, so I may be ready for my new beginnings.***"

We have chosen to be on the banks of the rushing McKenzie River. One minute the sun is shining through the new green leaves of May and raining on them the next. This is Oregon. This is coming home. The crossing of the Siskous was very extraordinary after being on the road for 9 months. The smell of the evergreens and the marvelous bright yellow Scotch Broom said 'Welcome home'. In all of our travels it seems to us that God did the one great job on Oregon. The thing I know about 'home' is that it varies for everyone. Home smells good, feels good, and soothes a deep place in the heart.

This is the end of a magnificent journey. I am so grateful for the ability to have made this trip, for safe travel, a loving mate, and two great traveling pets. This is an ending. It is good to remember to honor the ending and make ready for new beginnings. For us it is to open the mountain cabin, reconnect with friends and family and slide into a new beginning. Thank you God.

"Mourning the Past"

It seems to me there must be something called "soul-glue'. When it is time to move on from a place of joy even knowing that I will be back someday, a part of me mourns at a very deep level. I wonder if it is mourning the past or knowing that even in the returning it will never be the same.

It would seem that a 'soul' would be so evolved that it would never have to hold on to anything. But maybe the 'soul' is nothing more than our individual collective consciousness of many life times. Our current growth happens in a moment of God's grace when we see or feel at a deeper level. Each time during these periods of reflection, our soul will let in that brief instant of knowing.

This unexplainable feeling that it is time to go home, with no clue as to where home actually is, might just be our soul saying stop and savor this moment. While you might pass this way again in this lifetime or the next it will be different somehow. It would seem that the soul would only want to remember the quiet occurrences of God's grace.

Soul-glue is much more that letting go and letting God. It is our responsibility to remember in those times of mourning that we are so much more than this feeling. A time to know that our soul does go on and on and we need do nothing.

"Erase The Old Tapes"

It is always amazing to me how fast we can revert to old habits, ways or childhood behavior no matter how far we think we might have evolved on this spiritual journey. While we were on our nine-month sojourn around North America my sister came to visit. We had friends in the area and they invited us for dinner on Super Bowl Sunday. In the reading of this tale you must remember that now we have three people, one dog, and one cat in a 270 ft square space.

My sister was in the area where David was talking about the dinner plans. I was in the bedroom partially listening. I understood we would go, but not till later the next day. My sister understood we were not going. The next day my sister, our hostess, and I were talking. My sister told our hostess we were not coming. I said I didn't think that was correct. She insisted. This pushed some childhood buttons of the many times she thought she was right so I rushed off to find out from David whether we were going or not.

The point here is I rushed off like I was ten going to tattle to Mom or Dad. *Yeah*, I was right. How fast can we come back to sanity? My sister was hurt. The value in this tale is how quickly my sister identified and voiced her hurt, the way we were able to discuss it and my ability to make amends. **Thank you God for the opportunity to look at old negative tapes, you little tattle tail.**

"There is No Try"

Decision-making can be quite a process. I was in a holding pattern in my life: between relationships, living in a strange state, spelling regular caregivers for a weekend. It was Sunday and on the TV a person was talking about 'trying to go sit in a chair across the podium'. She would start to walk to the chair and then say, "Oh, what will my family think. I am too old. I might fail. It may not be a good financial investment. I might make a total fool of myself." She would then walk back to the lectern and start all over again 'trying'. Finally after much effort she said she could try until doomsday and not have it happen.

In the movie "Star Wars" Yoda says. "There is no 'try'."

WOW--the light went off in my head. What <u>was</u> my dream? What had I been trying to do? I wanted to do something that would allow me to be creative, independent and financially rewarded. ***I wanted to start my own business.*** After prayer and meditation I decided that a catering company would suit me just fine.

The first step was to make the commitment, so what was next? I had to get some cards printed and put the word out. First, I did the Thanksgiving dinner for the church. Then I got a job doing Thanksgiving dinner for a doctor and his family. Finally, I gave my cards out and I was launched. Thank you God, I had stopped 'trying'.

"Just Do It"

What keeps us from our dreams? As we traveled across the country during our nine-month sojourn, probably six out of ten people said that was their dream also. There were Canadians that wanted to travel across their country. Old and young alike said that was there dream. People in the gas stations would see the license plate and want to know where we were going and how far we had come. Many middle-aged children said they wish that their parents were doing something other then watching television and vegetating.

Conceive, believe and achieve is the answer. If a thought like getting a RV and traveling around the country comes into our heads, we can let the "yah buts" get a hold of us. "Yah but" I am whatever age. Ten years from now you will be ten years older and still not have lived your dream. Johnny Carson had a ninety-two year old man on his program several years ago and his dream was to travel to every state. His wife wouldn't do it. When she died he got a motor home and a younger companion and did it.

First comes the concept. Second the ability to believe that it can happen. The third thing is to take the first step however small. We started with the idea we would get a pop-up tent to do some camping. We then rented a class c (cab-over) to see if we liked it; finally the motor home. God helped us put our toe in the water and because we said, "YES", it has been a <u>great journey</u>.

"Terminal Potlucks"

All potlucks are not created equal! As a traveling minister and RVer I have to revisit this question. I have actually "flunked" potlucks for some time because I have to taste everything. There is also a part of me that wants to know if each person has contributed his or her share at a potluck. Sometimes I wonder if the food will hold out. Other times I remember a time when my father didn't think my mother was taking enough. Oh those old tapes get so tiresome. Those are the negative things about potlucks for me.

These are the positive things: In Hawaii, the diversity of the foods from the many cultures was exciting. The Philippines have a great dessert that's fried with sugar sprinkled. The Hawaiians have chicken long rice and poi. The Koreans would bring boi goi.

In churches, you have potlucks when visitors come and go, for holidays, and for any occasion under the sun. Once at the church in Hawaii we had four in one week causing the senior minister to note that he was glad that potlucks were not terminal.

The potlucks in the RV resorts on our trip across North American also had a great diversity to them. Once at a military "famcamp" we counted license plates from forty-two states. Thus we had a feast at the potlucks from East, West, North and South.

Thank you God that all potlucks are not created equal.

"God's Report Card

What kind of barometer do we have to measure how we are doing in life? It would be nice if God would give us an annual report card. Would we do or act differently if we got a C-minus in 'forgiveness'? Did we love unconditionally this year? How much judgment, fear, or criticism have I allowed in my life?

On our nine-month swing around North America I was always checking and examining what I was feeling and experiencing. It took me quite a period of time to realize that I wasn't having many mood swings. Things that might have upset me in the past seemed to float over my head. David and I were getting along famously. I was touched over and over again at how wonderful it was to observe our two pets up close and personal. The wonder of "talking story" with former classmates, friends, and best new friends was filled with great warmth. The joy of a second and third cup of coffee over a local paper added a new dimension.

One day I just looked at David and said, "I can't understand why I am so happy." What dawned on me was that my biggest thing to forgive was the man in the RV next to us who ran his electric cord across our space before we had moved up. I wasn't fearful of any thing it seemed. I had loved unconditionally most of the time. I guess just the realization of this was in fact God giving me a report card.

"What is Grace?"

What is God's grace? This was one of the big questions when I was going to seminary. It still was a big question seven years later when my husband went off to seminary. One of the professors made a statement while defining 'grace' indicating that you earned it. That was really challenged loudly by the students and after a long weekend and I am sure much reflection and prayer, she came back and retracted the statement. She might have been God's messenger to tell the class to revisit the question. The whole episode caused one to reexamine the question.

One of my favorite songs has always been 'Amazing Grace'. It always sounded better to me when you changed the word <u>'wretch' to 'soul'.</u> There is a mystery about 'grace'. Some magical clue takes us from being lost to being found. Anne Lamott says it nicely in her book <u>Traveling Mercies</u>, "the mystery of grace--meets us where we are but does not leave us where it found us."

There was a bumper sticker several years ago that said "Stuff Happens", but the good news is that grace happens also. The point is to be non-resistant and willing to accept the miracle of grace.

It would be nice if we could find grace whenever we wanted or needed it. Or maybe if we could accumulate points and earn a time when we would use grace at our own discretion. All I know is that when grace touches our lives we are profoundly aware and in awe.

"Pick Up Your Mat"

It seems this winter that so many friends and families are having health challenges. I called Silent Unity and put in several names. I know prayer works and the idea of continuous prayers for thirty days is really reinforcing. Recently I heard Father Leo Booth and realized again that there is no spot where God is not.

Father Leo said "If you are going thru the valley, don't stop; you don't have to build a house there." You can be sick for twenty years but it just takes one moment to heal. Maybe it won't be instant, but the healing idea has begun. We are three parts: body, mind and emotions.

On this spiritual journey we hear what we need to hear when we need to hear it or when we are willing. I had heard a great talk many years ago about the person by the bath in Bethesda for thirty-eight years. The first person that got in the pool when it began to roil was the one that was healed. The man on the mat had an excuse for all of those years. He couldn't get there first. He couldn't until he decided he COULD.

The physical part of life is about mind set. It's about affirming the positive and picking up your mat. I have lost thirty plus pounds. I am playing golf, walking, swimming, and playing tennis. I am writing. I am reading spiritual books. I am working on my own healing. Thank you God.

"Use Your Senses"

I awoke to the smell of earth and wet grass. It was one of the first nights that it was warm enough in January to leave the windows open. The early twilight sleep I was experiencing was delicious. I woke feeling grounded. I was grounded in gratitude and knowing I was right with the world.

Smell is just another God given sense that helps us remember the magnificence of the mystery of life. Smell is a great piece for me. I am sure each of us has one of the senses that is more developed then others. My husband's sense is the gift of sight. He chose to be an optometrist dealing with outer sight and then a Unity minister dealing with inner sight.

My sense of smell works wonders with cooking. I have always loved fragrances. I love to smell perfume and cologne on people. The smell of flowers wafting through the air reminds me again of the Master. When I lived on the farm I loved the smell of new mown hay. I also like the smell of it in the barn.

I can hardly wait to smell what this day has in store for me. Maybe today is the day to bake something. Maybe today is the day to stop and smell the flowers. Maybe today is the day to enjoy all the smells of shampoo and soap in the shower. Thank you God for your insightfulness into all of our senses as each one is awakening this day.

"It's History"

In Hawaii the Hawaiians know the importance of 'talking story'. The Native Americans had the talking stick. We recently got a gas outdoor fire pit. It is so great to sit around the fire and 'talk story'. There is something quite primal about it. We have the opportunity to listen a little deeper and share a little more of ourselves.

I realized the importance of history. It is really 'his story'. As we learn more about each other it becomes easier to love unconditionally. We have started asking a question at the close of the fire pit circle. Questions like: share something you learned today, what are you looking forward to, what issues are foremost on your mind, what are you grateful for today or what is your greatest accomplishment? If you want to be a rascal you could ask questions like: what don't you want to share with the circle or what is the most outrageous thing you have ever done? Laughter is a good thing and it can come from the circle.

These special times open the doors to the many ways we are alike plus wonderful information you would never have learned about the other people without this process. Whether it was our ancestors in wagon trains around a campfire or back in biblical times, the story is important. It is our history. It is "his story". The bible is our story. Let love flow through you as you make some new history today.

"Love of Life"

My father would start the beginning of the apple season saying that each variety of apple my mother made applesauce with was his favorite. He would have a second helping of fresh applesauce and proclaim it was the best. I often wondered how he could change his mind each time another variety ripened. The season started with an Oregon Transparent, followed by Kings, Granny Smiths, Delicious and others. It is so wonderful the way our judgments change as we get older.

I realized I had a similar affair with flowers. My first love was with pansies. I would study the different colors and pick out my favorite, quite sure that pansies were the most beautiful flower. Next were gardenias with the fragrance to dance to, with the white petals laid out in layers. After seeing a Georgia O'Keefe art show I became a fan of orchids. It was breathtaking to look down the deep throat to see the wonders they were hiding.

The current love is with the many colored poppies that are in the desert beds in the middle of winter. The petals look like material that would make a floating dress. The yellow center has such delicate pads for the insects to land on. I know I'm not fickle but snapdragons are just waiting for a closer look.

I guess whether it is applesauce or flowers there doesn't need to be a judgment about loving life. Plus there is always a new hybrid and have you tried Fuji's?

"Alligators of the Mind"

As I look across the small lake in front of the motor home, I see such tranquility and calm. It seems like my mind when I first wake in the morning and the brain waves haven't had a chance to go into overload.

This is the first lake we have stopped by in Southern Florida. The reflections of the motor homes across from us are silhouetted by the trees. The concern is alligators. I read the warning in the rules registration sheet. It says don't harass or feed the alligators. It goes on to say don't leave pets unattended. What a charming thought!

The only things I see in the lake this morning are turtles. As I sit and watch the lake come alive, I think of the alligators of my own mind. Where do the fears, concerns, and anxieties come from?

Are the mind alligators just lying dormant until I feed them? I can say to myself 'don't go there; don't feed that thought.' Some times it works and other times the "thought alligators" are just so hungry for some food. The trick is to not even give them a morsel.

Once I let a fear, concern or anxiety get a bite, it wants more food. For this day I will feed the beauty of the tranquility and the calm. If an alligator comes to the surface of my mind I will say not now I've got better things to do. I will just be in the 'now' and thank God for the beauty everywhere around me.

"Wonders Abound"

Something goes streaking through the house. My cat, Dim Sum, loves the morning. It is like she is celebrating the new day. She races from one end of our desert winter home to the other. Some times she stops and looks around to see if that pass managed to rouse anyone. Dimi can't understand why the dog, my husband or I aren't ready to greet this glorious day.

Now that I am up and look out the window from my computer I can see what she was excited about. The colors are changing from deep pinks to lighter colors. The breeze is fluttering gently in the tops of the palms. The light is only lighting their upper area. The golden colors from the morning sun are waking the palms from the top to the bottom. The palms show off their rings of life with the hacked off fronds from earlier years.

The bird sounds start to intensify. The very early walkers stride by with their long gaits. The flowers are waiting in the shadows for the desert sun to find them as it moves higher in the sky. The citrus trees hanging heavy with their winter bounty are also still waking and waiting for the morning sun to bath them in the warmth.

Thanks to all of the above, it must be time for my cup of coffee in the morning sun. A heart filled with gratitude for the gift of a new day. Thank you for another "Sonday".

"Extraordinary"

We recently saw a movie called 'All About Schmidt'. It was a great film. Jack Nicholson played the best role of his career. A local critic said it was about an ordinary person doing ordinary things in an extraordinary fashion. It was about the aging process, death, marriage, retirement, hope, relationships, and ordinary everyday events. The movie was cast with ordinary actors doing an extraordinary portrayal of "vanilla people" coping with ordinary issues. The movie appeared to be shot during a leafless rainy ordinary season in Omaha, Nebraska.

As an ordinary person living an ordinary life how can I perform extraordinary acts? The point being we just live our lives in love doing the best we can. We never know when some kind thing we say or do will touch or change someone else's life making the world just that much better.

For me at this time an important facet is each morning to ask God what it is for me to do this day. God can only do for us what he can do through us. I also like to move on whatever idea that comes up. The morning ordinary thought put into action just might turn out to be the extraordinary act of the day, week, month or year. Thank you God for this wonderful day. Thank you God for my body that functions in an extraordinary way. Thank you God for this extraordinary planet and every person, animal, plant, and thing.

"Woulda, Shoulda, Coulda"

The new book <u>The Power of Now</u> really touched me. We don't have to stay focused on the past or the future. We don't have to dwell on old hurts or resentments. The Now keeps us out of woulda, shoulda, and coulda disease. It is important that we learn from the past but we must let go if we are to move forward without blame and shame. I like to think we all do the best we can with the tools we have to work with, but it is time to move on.

I seem to be able to stay in the moment so completely that I can't remember that I made an appointment a few hours ago. We were in the process of selling our motor home and a lot at the same time. I was into overload. The realtor called and I said come by with the papers and about twenty minutes later I was off to the hot tub and showers, then returning in the Now to a message 'asking where was I?' The good news was I wasn't out to lunch so to speak. I was so totally in the moment all else slide by. Actually it is a little scary to be able to create such a vacuum in the mind and still stay in the moment.

It really is about staying in the moment even with phone calls from realtors. If I had been totally present during the call I **would** remember. Oh no, another form of woulda disease.

"Sonlight"

Winter morning walks in the desert are renewing and rewarding. The sunrises are always different in the way that they light the mountains. The morning sun has a unique way of backlighting the palm trees while it is pinking up the world in a 360-degree circle.

The light brings out all the canyons, ridges and peaks. The mountains look like they have frowns and wrinkles. The mountains are shaded in different hues like a great oriental print. The ones in the foreground are darker melting into lighter shades as the distance becomes greater. It is so easy to be awakened to the wonder and the beauty.

This is a time to awaken to the 'sonlight' as I walk in the morning 'sunlight'. God's awesome creation and light is shining into the valleys and low points in my life in a renewing fashion. On these morning walks it becomes easier to get my little life problems in the right order. They are really small in the larger picture. My morning mind set becomes more grateful and peaceful. It is in these times that I can do any forgiveness work and affirming for the coming day.

As the 'sonlight' lights my inside, the 'sunlight' is warming me through and through on the outside. My steps become lighter and before I know it I am singing. "This is the day that the Lord has made, let me rejoice and be glad in it."

"Is That It?"

The movie 'Kate and Leopold' is about a window in a time when they can move forward or back by hundreds of years. It is a cute movie; a love story and at the same time a thinky piece with many levels. At the end of the movie one person in the audience said rather loudly, 'Is that it?'

The movie makes one think about the courage and trust you would have to have to jump off a certain bridge at a particular time. On this spiritual journey there have been many times that I have tried to get others to jump into positive thinking. It took the right time and the right place for me. Why do I assume others would have the same courage and trust to cross over the bridge? How many times have I seen something and not been able to see the various levels?

It takes courage to leave old beliefs behind and trust that it will be better on the other side. What we don't know when we cross is, we can't go back and we can't get others to start the journey until they are ready. We can yell and wave but sometimes we have to let go. Knowing that the inner stirring and divine spark will give them a push when the courage and trust are there.

The different levels will be revealed and we won't have to ask, "Is that it?" The spiritual journey is never ending and is not for sissies.

"180 Degree Turn"

There are so many ways to see things in this lifetime. I like the ones that immediately show us we were 180 degrees off in our view. This makes me wonder how many times we aren't insightful enough to even notice. Two examples come to mind for me.

The first example was when I was a very young girl in the early 1940's. Our family was driving to the Oregon coast. The radio media was filled with anti-war slogans and stories of the enemy. My mother would spend time in a little tower not far from our house and observe planes. If one was sighted they would call and identify the direction and type of aircraft. The walls between the windows were filled with posters of various aircraft. I was in the back seat and saw this huge bomb. I started yelling hysterically and pointing but by that time it was behind a tree, **"WE are being bombed".** My parents finally got me quieted down and realized that I had seen my first blimp.

The second example was when my husband was in the shower and the dog jumped in with him. We had talked of giving Joy Luck a bath. David was so excited that his dog was so smart and wanted to take a shower with him. Ordinarily when you mention 'bath' she runs and hides. As he was toweling the dog down he heard the motivator: a beeping carbon monoxide alarm was going off and she was frightened. Thank you God for understanding and the ability to see things anew.

" Watch for Monkey Wrenches"

The wonderful French film 'Amelie' shows how people do the same thing over and over and expect different results. One man would sit in the cafe where much of the story took place, with a little recorder detailing what his former girlfriend was doing. Amelie's father was at a total loss after his wife's death. Amelie would do random acts of kindness and mischief to help them move on with their lives while she in fact seemed stuck in her own. Each character would continue the behavior that wasn't working for them.

The man in the cafe fell in love with a different girl in the cafe and after a very short period started keeping a recorder about her interaction with the other male customers. Amelie's father kept finding reasons for not traveling like he dreamed of. Amelie found an unlikely candidate to fall in love with and just continued to play games not meeting him. In the end because of all the things Amelie did, each person was able to cut to the chase.

I left the movie wondering again why it is so easy to see what others are doing to put a monkey wrench into their lives. But I did ask myself what is it I do that keeps me from playing the game of life full out? For this week I will be more aware of patterns that might be a monkey wrench in my life.

"Nothing is Lost in Spirit"

My husband David and I were returning from a long weekend on the island of Kauai. We had played some golf, walked on the beach and did some sightseeing. David had gone to get the car and I was to get the luggage together. Our first bags came off in a short time but no golf bags. I went up and down the carousels and checked the different areas thinking they might have came over on an earlier inter-island flight. No bags!

David arrived with the car and I put the luggage we had claimed in the car. I went back to check again. By now I knew that our golf clubs had been stolen. I stormed off to report it to the lost baggage people. I was describing the bags when a light went off. As I tried to remember when I saw them last I realized that they were still in the trunk of the rental car.

The amazing thing to me is how fast our mind can jump from reality to negativity. I know all about principle. I know nothing is lost in spirit. I also know how easy it is to jump to the worst case scenario.

The lesson for me is to watch how fast I can come back to center. The importance of remembering that God is in charge and only good can come to me. The car rental agency held our clubs for a few weeks until I had to go back to Kauai for a "HULA" MEETING. **H**AWAIIAN **U**NITY **L**EADERSHIP **A**SSOCIATION.

"JC Doesn't Play"

My beloved was following in my footsteps some seven years later experiencing a call to the ministry. We were living in the middle of America having arrived there from Hawaii. It was a spring weekend and we were going to play in a student golf tournament. The winter had been long and the warm spring sun most inviting. This would be the first golf game this year.

We were living in a three-story townhouse with very little storage. The golf clubs had been in the trunk of the car all winter or so we thought. David went out to get them out of the trunk and get them ready. No golf clubs. He came in and asked if I knew where they were. I told him to check the laundry room. No golf clubs. The clubs were nowhere to be found. We called the local police and reported that our clubs had been stolen. They came out and took a report.

My beloved was upset. That might be too mild a description of his pulling his hair and beating on his chest. I, being the senior minister and staying very calm, was feeling like it was time to let it go. I finally said with a 'judgmental superior than thou' attitude, "What would Jesus Christ do in a situation like this?"

My beloved husband said with out batting his eyes, "Carol Jean, Jesus Christ didn't play golf."

Thank you God for the lesson. But most of all thank you God for the wonderful gift of humor.

"One Liners"

My father used to have a one liner for everything. When I was growing up I learned them and tried to understand with my 'little mind" what they meant. "You take your own fun to the party", "Money doesn't grow on trees." and many more. My mother's big contribution was "always wear clean underwear in case you are in an accident."

My father was a logger and maybe for him money did grow on trees. I knew he meant money wasn't easy to come by as he lived through the depression. As a child I know for a while I looked at trees and wondered if they had ever grown money. I could imagine dollar bills hanging on the branches. All of this was with my 'little mind'. Now I have a "big mind" and I still love one-liners. They have changed.

These are some of my favorite new one-liners: "God is so good", "Peace be still", "There is no spot where God is not", and "Thank You God". In trying times I only seem to be able to get my mind around a small lifeline that is really very, very big. No matter the incident, God help me to see the good in this. No matter the storm in or around me, let me get still in my mind. No matter where I am or what I am about, God is everywhere present. To always remember to say, "thank you God" for my many blessings in life. Thank you father and thank you Father.

"Laughter Gets You Through"

Our North America swing for nine months in the motor home allowed us to visit many Unity Centers. They have a wide range, probably like all denominations. The third Sunday of Advent we happened on to 'thee' most **high;** High being very structured, formal and quite proper. It was mostly a music program and the selection reminded my husband David of songs he had heard as a child in Cleveland. Having to be proper in church had long since left both of our pictures.

Of course it was easy to compare this to the previous Sunday when the place buzzed with energy and interaction before the service. We had had lunch with the minister and she had given us a grand tour of her city. The exchange was warm and friendly. Oh my, why do we have to compare?

About half way through the service, David, who was sitting on the aisle, dropped his program. A few minutes later in a very quiet somber moment he dropped his hard glass case. It seemed to hit on the uncarpeted floor very loudly. He just left it there for a while. I leaned over and asked him "Are you having a spell?" His face got red as he smothered his laughter. Occasionally during the rest of the service we would glance at each other and have to stifle our amusement.

God does have such a grand sense of humor. Thank you God for the ability to laugh and see the joy in small everyday things.

"Be Gentle"

It is really fun to awaken to how much one has **not** evolved on this spiritual journey. I was living in Hawaii during the time my parents were going through the last years of their lives and consequently my sister did most of the care giving.   Years have past and my husband David and I are in our motor home on our North American sojourn.

It is Christmas time and we are parked in the side yard of David's only sibling. Ten months ago his sister had a stroke. She is doing better than we could have imagined. She has caregivers come in to help. Here in lies the lesson. During the few days we were there, her only son flew in and so with all of us there she cancelled the daily help.

I watched myself be little. Her condition pushed my own mortality buttons and I developed an attitude. When I finally woke up to my attitude I affirmed in my morning meditation "I am a gentle, caring, giving person who creates memories for others." How does one create memories for others? By realizing that this was an opportunity to see the Christ Presence in someone else and to let my own Christ Presence come to the surface.

The memories were celebrating the Christ by foot massage, gentleness and being aware of what it must be like to function with only one arm. Also celebrating the Christ in my own sister and all the selflessness she portrayed with our parents. Thank you God.

"Thanks for the Message"

One of my very favorite professors while I attended seminary was Maurice. We had also become prayer partners. Each morning at 6 AM one or the other of us would call and we would read some inspirational material and then affirm for each other what we wanted to co-create with God for that day. This was life-changing stuff.

The connection between us was deepened when Maurice picked up the phone and called my oldest son who was having a kidney transplant. Maurice had received a kidney from his brother while he was in seminary. Once my husband and I had run into Maurice at the airport as all of us headed off for a Unity cruise. Maurice's favorite aunt was very ill. I helped him remember that God is in charge and it is OK. We then sat in a circle and prayed together.

One day I received a call saying Maurice's kidney had failed again and he was no longer physically on this planet. A few days later my husband and I were in our computer room reading and sending emails. I was writing to a friend and told her of Maurice's death. I said that a great thread had been removed from the human tapestry. At that moment a music box that was broken and hadn't played for a long time began to play *Laura's Theme*. Maurice had always told us he wanted a relationship like David and I have. Thank you Maurice for telling us one last time.

"Wake Up"

I am back. Where do I go when I stop writing and expressing myself through words? I don't even know when it stops or what prompts it. After many months I realize that I have stopped something very good. What are my excuses? Why have I fallen asleep?

Was it when I found 'Pogo.com' games on the computer? I like to think I am exercising my brain and that it is a form of meditation. My brain waves seem to move into an Alpha state. Did someone say something to me that made me hook in once again to the belief that I have nothing to share or have poor writing skills?

I have lots of questions and no answers. Maybe my soul is gathering. Gathering my next spurt of creativity. I am awake in some areas of my life because I am almost to my Weight Watcher goal and am doing regular walking.

Today I started the day at 6:30 AM with a walking photo shoot. It was like my eyes were opened once again. It was easy to see God everywhere present. The mother ducks on the pond with their new flock. The flowers ending the desert winter felt like fall, as the hot summer planting of zinnias begins. Thank you God; I know you are always here. It is I who forgets and goes to sleep for a brief period of time. It is always wonderful to 'come home' once again, just one step closer to you God.

"Beauty at the Ballet"

Today as I heard the words of "In This Very Room", they had a new meaning. "In This Very Room" there is quite enough joy, love, peace, etc. I felt all of the above. The new thought was that when we are in a place that is filled with positive ions, we breathe them. It becomes like a contagious happening. The feeling is beautiful. There is quite enough air.

If this is so then the opposite of that is true. We must always be aware of the negative and destructive. The evening news, the daily papers, the "gloom and doom" friends or relatives can be contagious. It is our job to take the destructive and re-construct it to create our world. We don't have to become Pollyannas. The balance between holding the higher watch and accepting the "ain't it awful" is a narrow walk.

We have a friend who stood up with David and me when we got married. He is an actor and director in Copenhagen. We had the good fortune of going to the ballet with him. As we looked around at all the beautiful people, he assured us that not 'everything was beautiful at the ballet'. It is good to remember we don't have to know it all.

Holding the higher watch through God can help to change the picture. What ever or where ever the room, it is important to breathe in the joy, love, and peace because it is contagious.

"He Watches Me"

The days are getting more and more "fall like" in the Pacific Northwest where we spend our summers. One of the ways I know is that the cat decides to come to the loft to sleep. At first she just lays on the floor and I almost step on her night after night. I moved her bed box up by my bed, but she just comes and smells it. However by morning she has found her place in the box.

This is really a delightful feeling for me. I spend some warm moments just looking at her in her sleeping state. She likes to lay on her head in a most uncomfortable position. I asked my self, does she _hear me watching_. Maybe she would sense I love looking at her. No response. Dimi kitty was in her own place of peace and total bliss.

I wondered how we know if we are being watched over. I couldn't help but equate it to how often we might be aware of someone lovingly watching over us. Do we _hear Him watching us_? I love it in the moment I remember that God is everywhere present. This to me is a warm loving feeling of God's grace.

In times of stress or anxiousness I ask God to watch over my loved ones and me. This is usually around travel or sometimes at bedtime. My new goal is to be aware of the closeness of God in all my affairs: the wonder of taking the time to hear Him watch me. Thank you God for this awareness.

"Dump the Baggage"

My walking buddy Dee and I share many, many deep subjects on our morning walks. We talk about our past, our kids, our husbands, about the joy of sharing our spiritual journeys, etc. She is like a sponge: Curious, open, willing to learn and grow in whatever way she can.

I find that a week or two later she will expound on a point I might have made. It's like watching a duckling taking to the water or a baby bird on first flight. She is ready to be rid of any baggage that isn't serving her now. Like so many of us in the beginning of this spiritual exploration, she wants it yesterday. "What books should I read? Am I meditating in the right way?" I assure her this is all in good time. There is no special book and no special way to meditate.

As she has left more and more of the unnecessary baggage behind, she is feeling lighter and lighter. On our morning walks we see slugs that labor so slowly across the road. On their backs at the very end, they pick up a large supply of fir needles and baggage. Dee has taken it upon herself to gently step on the stuff until they shed their heavy load and move in a shining line on across the road. As the slug moves on his way much lighter, it doesn't even know that a larger than life angel has just helped it lighten the load.

God helps us on our journey when we are willing to let go and let God help us shed our baggage.

"A New Page"

It's a new day. It's a new blank page. It's a new thought. It's a new story. How wonderful that we have the amazing opportunity to start a new! If each morning we had to start with the same old, same old that wouldn't be very exciting. There is a charming song that states, "Everything much change nothing stays the same". Every morning can seem like it is much the same and yet; it is never the same.

Life is in the little changes. Life is in being awake to the smallest wonder. Life is about knowing that God is right in the middle of the change and yet is always the constant.

Routine can be so boring if we let it. I like to swim with a mask and snorkel when I do laps. One morning I became aware of the rainbows that were forming on the bottom of the pool from my arms breaking the surface. It was like a kaleidoscope; diamond shapes moving, changing with the rainbows defining the edges. They had always been there when the light was just right but my awareness had not. They were not in both direction, so on each turn I had a gift of rainbows waiting for me. By looking for the wonder, the morning had become a wonder.

Today I begin a new. For me this day there is no same old, same old. I awaken to the beauty and surprises all around. Thank you God for all things new and wondrous.

"Full Computer"

The older I get the more annoying it is to forget names, places, and happenings. I like to beat myself up and say, "Oh, it's just a Saddlebrooke moment." Saddlebrooke just happens to be when I live in the winter. I noticed that I have the same lapses when I go north in the summer. It isn't just a Saddlebrooke moment or a senior moment it is a occurrence that comes with packing our mind with countless information.

My friend Cheryl, was very concerned she was losing it at age sixty. She spoke to her doctor about it and he assured her that our brain is like a computer and if we have sixty years of files and folders it can take a bit to pull up the information. This was a most assuring proclamation. It would be good if the brain didn't have to process the data at 3 AM in the morning.

If we stay focused in the present moment it does help to remember what is going on. It is when we drift off to the past or the future that we can't remember what is going on in the present. I once heard a Kuhana in Hawaii say, "The past is history and the future a mystery, but the gift is in the moment and that is why we call it the PRESENT.

Paul said: "Forgetting that which is behind I press on toward the high goal of Christ in me."

"Chose Happy"

It is so easy to say 'Chose Happy' but sometimes it takes a cattle prod to make this happen. What does it mean to say these words? It seems to say that when the abyss is looming on the horizon and our attitude is going in the wrong direction, we are at choice.

One rainy day in Oregon soon after our arrival back from the sunny Southland of Tucson, I didn't want to get out of bed because my walking partner was out of town and the rain was pounding hard on my sleeping loft. I know how important exercising is for me and I could feel myself falling down the pit of gloom. I had a day to choose what I was going to do. I was choosing unhappy, gloom and doom, and poor little old me. Now what!!

How long do I want to stay in this funk? Is it serving me in some way I am not even aware of? What are my choices for this day? The first thing that came to me "was you are bright enough to chose again." This comes from the 'Course in Miracles'. Each fork in the road gives us the opportunity to choose once again. With this knowledge, I might as well 'Chose Happy". Besides it is so much nicer for all of those around us.

I chose to make a list.

- ☺ Remember God is in this with me.
- ☺ This too will pass.
- ☺ As I climb out of the pit, celebrate.
- ☺ Do a hallelujah dance and a thank you God.

"Breathe the Smell"

What is that wonderful smell? It's the freshness of the rain on the Douglas fir, the cedars, the cottonwoods, and the ferns and moss. The smell of the forest carpet as my feet grind the fir needles and release the heavenly smell.

What is that wonderful smell? It's the smell of fresh baked bread, cinnamon rolls, or pie. This kind of smell starts my taste buds salivating. It can also bring up memories of when I was young and the smells from the kitchen meant safety and home.

What is that wonderful smell? It's the smell of new mown hay or lawn. There is also a promise of the smell of summer or harvest in these smells. There is also the smell of fresh sweat from the work of the harvest or just plain yard work.

What is that wonderful smell? It's the cologne of a loved one and the promise of commitment and the future. The smell of baby powder or oil on a baby as the bonds grow deeper with each breathe. With all the life and love to come from the innocence of the above.

What is that wonderful smell? It's the smell of freshly laundered sheets that have been dried in the summer sun. The emotions that everything is in divine order as you tiredly slide beneath the sheets at the end of a perfect day. All of this if we just stay conscious to our breathe.

"Carry Twigs"

This being a 'Snow Bird" has it's ups and downs. For those of you that don't know, a 'Snow Bird' is someone that splits their time between North in the summer and South in the winter. In our case it is Oregon in the summer and Arizona in the winter.

This means readying each place for departure and arrival. What clothes do I have in which place? How to empty the freezer and refrigerator in a timely fashion? Remembering to change the phones, stop the paper, address changes , etc . You get the picture.

Upon arrival back in Oregon this time we had major water problems. A leak under the kitchen sink, a leak at the washer and many hot tub issues. After cleaning the hot tub and filling it with 400 gallons of water, it turned brown on the third day. The brown condition is discovered as we stand in our swimsuits ready to take the cover off and get in the tub.

Then we drive to the closest area to get chlorine, new coffee pot, and cushions for outdoor chairs. Fly this way and that with 'twigs in your mouth' making our current nest wonderful one more time. Take back coffee pot, it makes too much noise and pours funny. Take back cushions they don't fit.

Dear God thank you for the energy and strength to fly with these 'twigs' as we make it all wonderful. A nest where we pray, say thank you and live in serene peace.

"Slow Down"

How many times have we heard 'It's not the destination; it is the journey? Yet we start out by wanting to get our drivers license the minute we are the right age. Then it might be to have the first drink when we are a legal age. Rush, rush, rush to what? Some times when we get there, wherever 'there' is, it's not what we hoped for. The joy was actually in the getting there, not the there.

We need to think about how much unhappiness and disease we cause ourselves by being in a rush or hurry to have something happen or to get something done. Sporadically we need to stop and rest, pause and ask ourselves 'What is going on here'? Am I finding joy in this rat race? I can see myself sometimes like a hamster in a cage; the faster I run the faster I have to keep running. It doesn't take long in this mode before you become irritable, tired and unreasonable.

Amalie Frank, my mentor, use to say, 'Life lived by the yard is hard, life lived by the inch is a cinch'. Alcoholics Anonymous says, 'One day at a time, one step at a time'. To stay happy, healthy and whole we must take time to remember to slow down. Take time to meditate, daydream, or whatever if is that refreshes your soul. When the soul is refreshed we can see the world with different lenses and begin anew.

"Plant Seeds"

The weather was awesome. Something deep inside me said 'plant a garden'. Well maybe not a whole big plot like my Dad would do, but some herbs and a few hills of cucumbers and zucchini. Before I could even get the ground ready, it started to rain. I knew it would be better to wait a few days because it was really cooling off, but my excitement wouldn't let me.

The weather continued to be bad and everyday or two I would go look to see if the seeds were sprouting up through the dark soil. I actually thought of digging down a little to see what was happening. Now I know this would disrupt the growth and progress, so I refrained myself. As I write it is still raining and no sprouts. Maybe they are drowning in the Oregon May weather!

This is a lot like the spiritual seeds that get planted in our mind. We plant them and then think they should bear immediate fruit. We also think we can plant fear, worry, lack and hate seeds and get prosperity, peace, love, and serenity. We create the climate for a good crop with positive thoughts, inspirational book sand music.

It is important to be disciplined in our daily prayer and meditation. Be patient. Be grateful. Remember not to expect corn or beans if you plant cucumbers and zucchini. As the negative seed attempts to grow in our minds we have to be conscious enough to say, "You're not the seed I choose to plant, Thank You God."

"Slowly Die"

As I sit on my balcony at a resort in San Carlos, Mexico, the world doesn't get much better. The palm trees are in the foreground with bright colored birds singing and going about their morning rituals and tasks. My rituals and tasks have changed this morning and I don't have any thing to do right now but be still and see the beauty and God's messages all around me.

The morning sun is just breaking on the rock formation on my right. This area is on the Sea of Cortez and the morning sun is to my back as I look across this huge water to the Baja. It is not visible but I know it's there. It is nice to just be at such a deep level of peace and contentment.

A sailboat is moored out by the rock formation. The occupants are just starting to stir with their morning household tasks. If I were closer I know I could smell coffee and bacon wafting across the still ocean. The ocean is flat with faultless formations of pelicans waiting for the lighting to be better for their morning dives to the ideal breakfast. A whole fish wiggling down their throat slowly dying for their survival.

What is it that we slowly die to so something else may live in this chain of survival called life? Maybe it is in our living that others thrive and grow on this spiritual journey called life. It could also be in the awareness that comes when we really see the wonder and beauty around us.

"Different Strokes"

While I lived in Washington, D.C. early on my spiritual journey, I liked to go to both services at my beloved Rev. Amalie Frank's church and then race down town and go to Rev. Lafyette Seymour's later service. I just couldn't get enough in my spiritual pouch. Later I learned the name for people like me is 'spiritual bliss bunnies'. I was sure I had found the total answer.

It is really easy to assume that the path I had recently found was the journey for everyone. Not only the path but my church on Capital Hill. On a trip to my second church one Sunday I saw one of the church board members joining the downtown church. Oh my gosh, this is awful. What a novice I was on this spiritual journey! Later I learn that I could not judge another's needs, route or place for their particular path.

There are not only many different religions, various denominations and different churches in the world but diverse paths for each person. The soul has to discover the way and there are different strokes for different folks. We can encourage each other and set an example by our own journey but there are as many different paths to God as there are people on this planet. The 'bliss bunny' has slowed down now and realizes that the important thing is to say 'Namaste' to each person we meet. I behold the Christ in you and I honor you for who you are and where you are on your spiritual journey.